09-BUC-745

TABLE OF CONTENTS

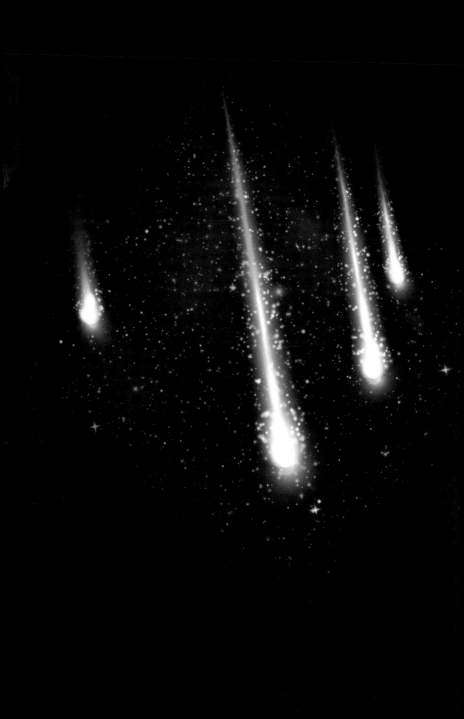

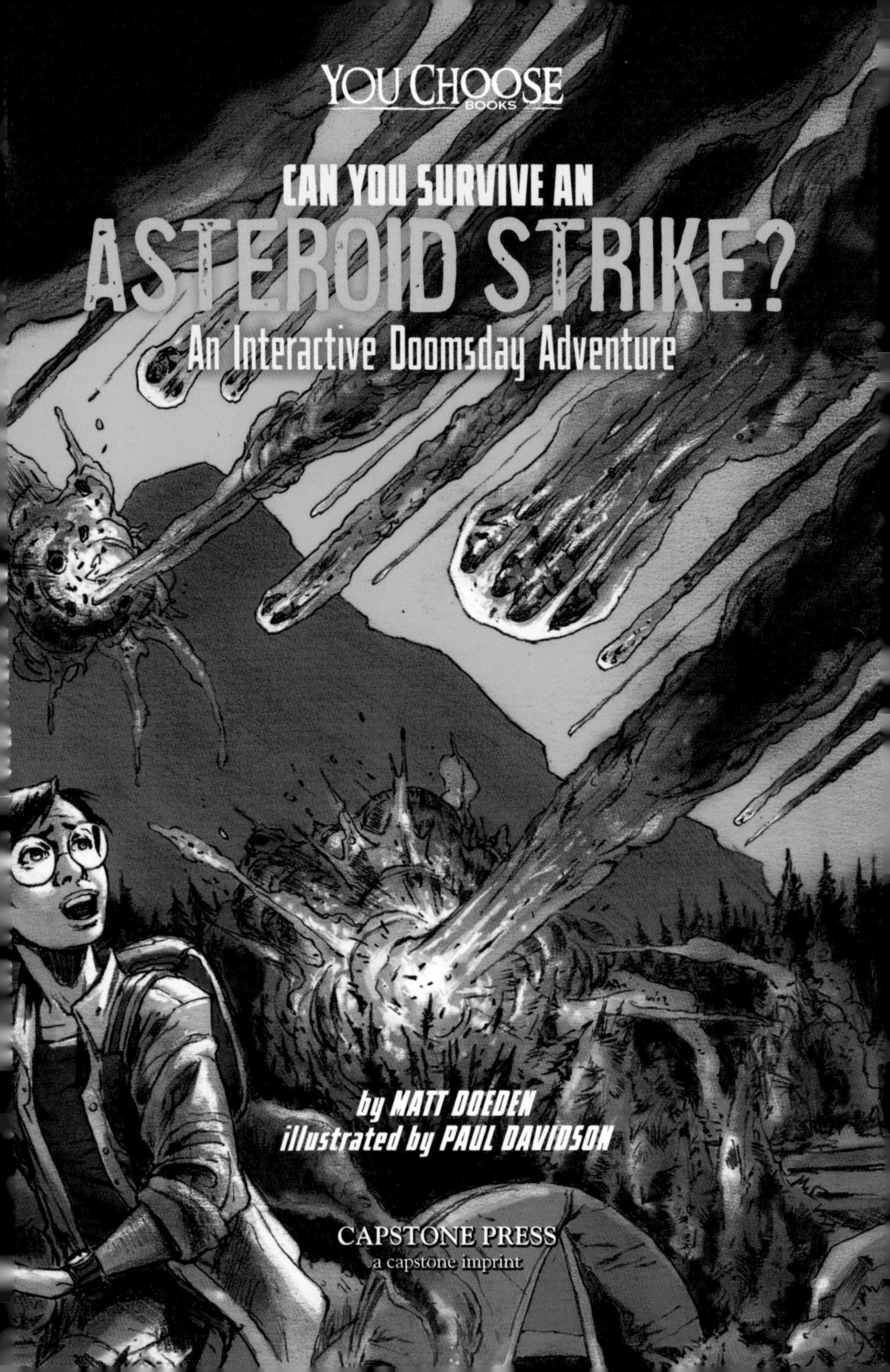

YOU CHOOSE BOOKS

CAN YOU SURVIVE AN ASTEROID STRIKE?

An Interactive Doomsday Adventure

by MATT DOEDEN
illustrated by PAUL DAVIDSON

CAPSTONE PRESS
a capstone imprint

You Choose Books are published by Capstone Press,
1710 Roe Crest Drive, North Mankato, Minnesota 56003
www.mycapstone.com

Library of Congress Cataloging-in-Publication Data
Cataloging-in-publication information is on file with the Library of Congress.
ISBN 978-1-4914-8109-7 (library binding)
ISBN 978-1-4914-8127-1 (paperback)
ISBN 978-1-4914-8133-2 (eBook PDF)

Editorial Credits
Anthony Wacholtz, editor; Bobbie Nuytten, designer;
Jo Miller, media researcher; Gene Bentdahl,
production specialist; Nathan Gassman, creative director

Photo Credits
Shutterstock: Lonely, (background, throughout), Igor Zh, 102

Printed in US.
007528GCS16

ABOUT YOUR
ADVENTURE

YOU are living through a worrisome time in the future of humanity. An enormous asteroid is on a collision course with Earth. As everyone scrambles for safety, can you keep your wits and do what it takes to survive? Start your adventure by turning the page, then make your choices as you go along. Every decision you make will affect how your story unfolds. Do you have what it takes to survive the impending colossal impact?

YOU CHOOSE the path you take through an Asteroid Strike.

FIRE FROM THE SKY

You wake with a start. Sirens ... voices ...
shouting. Footsteps thunder on the floor above
you. You sit up on the motel bed, rubbing your eyes.
What's happening?

You step to the window and throw open the ugly
floral-patterned drapes. Outside, people are running
and shouting. Car horns blare out. Is that a tornado
siren wailing in the distance? You notice that your
parents' car isn't in their spot. That means they're still
sightseeing in the city.

You turn and grab the remote for the TV. A news
program is showing a photograph. At first, it just
looks like a random smudge of light in the night sky.

" ... according to NASA, the asteroid is about 8
kilometers across," says a woman's voice. "It will strike
somewhere in the North Atlantic at 9:01 p.m. Eastern
Standard Time tomorrow."

Turn the page.

Your knees go weak, and you collapse onto the bed. For the next several minutes, you stare at the screen, watching and listening with a sense of numb disbelief.

You change the channel. Another station shows a news anchor interviewing a man identified as Dr. Grady, an astrophysicist at Stanford University.

"How bad will this be?" asks the news anchor. "Aren't we lucky that it's hitting water instead of land?"

"No, no, no," says Grady. "If anything, that's worse. You have to understand, this impact will affect everyone on Earth. It will create a tsunami 1 to 2 kilometers high. It will set off massive earthquakes worldwide, which will cause even more tsunamis."

The news anchor's face goes white. "So people need to get to high ground to be safe?"

Grady sighs. "In the short term, I suppose so. But understand, this changes everything. Flaming debris raining down everywhere. Massive earthquakes rocking the entire planet. Rock, dust, and steam blanketing Earth. We're talking about nuclear winter. Little or no sunlight getting through for years."

Grady leans forward in his chair. "Understand this. The world as we know it ends tomorrow. Civilization will fall. Most of the world's species will be extinct within a few months. And that may include us."

The remote slips from your hand. You sit in stunned silence for a few moments. Then you reach for your phone to call your parents. But you don't have any service. The lines are probably overloaded.

Turn the page.

You glance at the map that sits on the nightstand. You're staying in a little motel about 20 miles west of Washington D.C., near Dulles Airport. You and your parents have been touring the East Coast of North America for the past month. Today, the plan was to hit up the National Mall in Washington D.C. But this morning, you weren't feeling well and decided to go back to sleep.

It's only 20 miles. But now, with highways jammed and phones down, it's almost like they're a world away. You run again to the window. To the east, the Appalachian Mountains rise above the landscape. High ground. It might be your best shot—your only shot—at survival. But if you go that way, even if you leave a note, what are the odds you'll ever see your parents again?

To head for high ground, go to page 11.
To make plans to reunite with your parents,
turn to page 14.

You can almost hear your dad's voice. Get somewhere safe! Waiting here, or even worse, going to the city, would be suicide. You hold out hope that you all will survive and meet again. Right now, you focus on getting out of the path of the tsunami.

You cram everything you have into your backpack. A flashlight, two bags of trail mix, a change of clothes, a warm sweatshirt, some beef jerky, and every water bottle you can find.

The last thing you grab is a map of the area. It's about 60 miles west to the Blue Ridge Mountains. That's your goal. Your watch reads 12:38. You've got a day and a half to cover the distance.

With your pack over your shoulder, you cross the motel parking lot with no plan other than to keep going west. Around you, the world seems to be going mad. Roads are gridlocked as people try to flee. Emergency sirens blare from all directions. People run through the streets. It's a full-fledged panic.

Turn the page.

You follow highway 29 out of Centreville, just a few miles south of Dulles. Above, the sky is filled with planes and helicopters. All of them are headed west.

A teenage boy whizzes by you on the shoulder riding a purple mountain bike. You stare after him jealously. A sturdy bike could be the difference between living and dying.

Half a mile up the road, you hear groaning coming from a stand of nearby trees. You step off the shoulder to investigate and notice the flash of purple in a bush. It's the bike! A few feet away, the boy lies in a heap. Blood streaks his face, and he's holding his left leg.

"Are you okay?" you ask, stepping closer.

He moans. "Hit a rock. Wiped out, hard." His leg is badly broken, twisted and with bone sticking out of the skin. You feel the blood draining from your face.

"It's bad," says the boy weakly. "I know what this means. I'm done. Take the bike. Get somewhere safe."

To take the bike, turn to page 18.
To help the boy, turn to page 24.

You can't bear the thought of never seeing your parents again. You know they were headed to the National Mall to see the Washington Monument and the White House. You start cramming everything you have into your backpack, set on hiking the 20 miles or so to downtown D.C. But before you leave, good sense gets the better of you. Your parents know you're here. They may be coming back this way already. The smart play is to stay put.

Waiting makes for a long, miserable day. The news is almost too depressing to watch. The scene outside isn't much better. Streams of people are fleeing west. Tempers are running short. You hear more than a few rounds of gunfire. You find yourself checking the window every few minutes. Day stretches into evening. The evening turns into a long, restless night. By morning, you can't wait for your parents any longer. It's time to go find them.

The Metro would normally be the quickest way into the city. But one look at the street tells you that the trains aren't operating. It's likely they were overrun, or that Metro employees simply fled the city.

In the parking lot, a family is loading their things into the back of a small sedan. A boy, maybe 8 years old, is crying. "We don't have room for your scooter," his dad scolds. "Forget it. We need to go, now!"

The small motorized scooter tips over as the car roars out of the parking lot. You move fast, scooping it up. You're in luck—the battery is charged!

Turn the page.

The scooter's little motor whines as you take off east. The main roads are packed bumper to bumper. Horns blare. You know it won't be long before desperation turns people violent. You stick to sidewalks and side streets as much as you can, weaving your way east. It's a little more than 20 miles from your motel to downtown.

The scooter gets you about half that distance before the battery dies. You ditch the little machine and continue on foot. Morning turns into afternoon, and the sun grows hotter by the hour.

As you approach the Potomac River, you hear shouting. A man in a suit and tie kneels outside the U.S. Marine Corps War Memorial, clutching his leg. "Help me!" he calls. "Can anyone help me?"

To see if you can help, turn to page 26.
To continue to the National Mall, turn to page 29.

You glance again at the boy. His face is twisted in pain. The leg looks awful. He needs a doctor, now. But that's not going to happen. In any other situation, you'd do everything you could to help. But you can't help him, and stopping now just means you'll be dead too.

"Thanks," you say. "I'm sorry." You almost ask the boy for his name but realize that you don't want to know it. Fighting back tears, you climb onto the mountain bike, adjust your backpack, and start to ride. You pretend not to hear the boy's muffled sobs as you ride away.

The rest of the day is a blur. Major highways are at a standstill, so you make your way by back roads. Streams of people flee on foot, on motorcycles, and on bikes. You even see some riding horses through the chaos.

As you ride down a little-used back road, keeping your distance from the madness of the major highways, you come upon a large group of bicyclists. Most of the riders appear to be about college age.

To approach the group, go to page 19.
To turn around to find a different route, turn to page 23.

You're out here by yourself, with no real survival strategy beyond just trying to make it to the mountains. You need a group, and these people look as likely as any to take in a kid. You move carefully, calling out as you approach. You don't want to startle anyone—especially if they have weapons.

"Hello!" you call, waving both arms to make it clear you're unarmed.

"Hello there," comes the answer. A young man on an orange mountain bike drops back to greet you. "Nice ride there," says the man, nodding at your bike.

"Thanks," you answer, shuddering at the thought of how you got it. "Where are you going?"

Turn the page.

"Name's Hassan. Just trying to get out of that wave's path, really. There were just a few of us when we started. We go to college ... erm, I guess we went to college together. Anyway, we knew the roads would be jammed, and that bikes might be the best option. So we just started riding. The group has grown since we left. Those who can keep up are welcome. Safety in numbers, right? There are people out there who would kill you for that bike right now. A solid mountain bike is worth more today than a Porsche!"

You tell Hassan of your idea to flee to Shenandoah National Park. But he has other plans. "Shenandoah might not be far enough. Last projections I saw, the waters are going to reach as far inland as the Blue Ridge. That's cutting it too close for my taste. We're going to the far side of the Allegheny Mountains, to Monongahela National Forest."

Turn the page.

"Wait—how far is that?" you ask.

"We plan to skirt the mountains to the north, then double back around."

"That has to be 100 miles!"

Hassan shrugs. "Probably a bit more, by my best guess."

You look at your watch. It's past 7 p.m. More than 100 miles, much of that hard climbing, in a single day? You've already had a hard day of riding, you're still not feeling well, and you're not sure it's possible.

"You're welcome to come, but if you can't keep up, we won't wait." With that, Hassan rides on ahead.

To continue with the group bound for Monongahela National Forest, turn to page 30.
To break away and head the shorter distance to the Blue Ridge Mountains, turn to page 36.

You've seen enough disaster movies in your time to know that the only thing more dangerous than the asteroid is other people. What if they're armed? What if they steal your bike—or worse? It's possible that they're friendly, but is it really worth the risk?

You pull your bike to a stop and watch the group of riders pull away. They never even notice you.

You turn around and backtrack, finding another route east. You're rumbling down a little-used dirt road as sunset approaches. You hear a sickening *hissssss*, and then the bike jumps out beneath your feet. It skids out from under you, sending you sprawling onto the hard dirt below. Sure enough, the front tire is punctured. A nail is lodged in the tread. And you have no way to fix it.

You look around and see a red barn in the distance. It might be a good place to spend the night. That is, if you think you can afford to stop for the night.

To go to the barn, turn to page 66.
To continue on foot through the night, turn to page 71.

If you had broken your leg, you would want someone to help. You take a deep breath, step forward, and introduce yourself. "What's your name?"

"Rasheed," the boy groans.

"Rasheed, I'm not leaving you here. You need a doctor." You kneel down, unfold your map, and trace the road with your finger. "We must be about half way between Warrenton and Amissville," you say. "Any idea if either of those towns have a hospital?"

Rasheed glances at the map. "I'm sure Warrenton does. That's a good-sized town. Amissville is pretty small." He winces. "But I've never been there."

You turn and look over your shoulder. "Okay then."

Rasheed grabs your arm. "But wait. Warrenton is the wrong way. We'd be going east instead of west. That's the not the direction to be going right now."

He's right. The idea of backtracking makes you nervous. Rasheed looks to you to make a decision.

To head back to Warrenton, turn to page 40.
To continue west toward Amissville, turn to page 41.

"What's wrong?" you ask, approaching. The man is in his early 60s, and his face is covered in sweat.

"I'm trying to get to the White House," he says. "Twisted my ankle. It's bad."

"I'm going that way," you answer, introducing yourself and extending a hand.

The man shakes it. "Thank you so much. I'm Ed. Ed Tanner."

You pause. "Ed Tanner?" you repeat. You know that name. Now that you look closer, the face is familiar too. "You mean Speaker of the House Ed Tanner?"

"That's me," he says with a smile. "But you can just call me Ed."

The two of you continue east, at a much slower pace. You glance at your watch. Less than four hours until impact. "You're one of the most powerful people in the country," you say. "How come you don't have your own car? Or helicopter. Or something?"

Ed waves his cell phone. "Lines are jammed."

The two of you trudge on. You tell him about your quest to find your parents, about how finding them is the most important thing to you. You keep talking to keep his mind off the pain.

The National Mall is a sea of bodies. People line the sidewalks. Some are singing. Others are shouting or waving signs. You read a few:

"NASA Will Save Us!"

"Behold the Wrath of God!"

"Take Me to Your Bunker!"

You weave through the crowds, all the while helping to support Ed's weight. You're just north of the Washington Monument—a few blocks from the White House—when someone in the distance catches your eye. It's just a fleeting glance, but you see flowing dark hair and a floral-print dress—just like the one your mother was wearing. Your heart skips ... could it have been her?

To help Ed the rest of the way, turn to page 37.
To leave Ed and chase after the woman, turn to page 91.

You glance at your watch. Less than six hours until impact. A lot of people need help right now, but there's nothing you can do. You forge ahead, wading through an ever-increasing mass of people.

As you near the mall, you notice an increasing military presence. Armed soldiers stand on corners. Army vehicles line the streets. You realize they may be all that's preventing the city from falling into chaos.

As you're looking at a pair of soldiers standing at the next corner, someone taps your shoulder. "Hey," says a teenage boy, maybe a year or two older than you. "I'm Hank. That's Sean. See that Army Jeep up there?"

"Yeah, what about it?"

"We're gonna steal it. That thing can run off-road, no problem. It's our only way out of here."

"And why are you telling me?"

"We need a distraction. Get those guards' attention. Let us grab the Jeep and be ready to jump on. You in?"

To help them steal the Jeep, turn to page 84.
To decline the offer, turn to page 86.

It's a brutal ride. The group takes a few hours overnight to rest. But as exhausted as you are, you can't sleep. Then, long before dawn, it's back on the road. As you skirt north of the Blue Ridge Mountains, the terrain gets rougher. For miles at a time, the group is forced to walk the bikes up steep slopes.

By evening of the following day, you're dizzy from hunger and exhaustion. Your hands tremble. You can barely feel your legs, and what you can feel is pure pain. But you made it. You and the rest of the group—the ones that made it, anyway—are huddled atop a remote western peak of the Allegheny Mountains. Hassan seems certain that the wave won't reach you here.

"According to NASA, the asteroid should be coming down any second now," says Hassan.

When it finally happens, the entire earth seems to convulse. Winds howl. Within a few minutes, the first of the flaming debris begins to rain down from the sky. You hold your breath, dreading the enormous wave. Minutes pass. Five. Ten. Twenty. Thirty.

Turn the page.

It never comes—you made it far enough inland. You let out a long breath and fight back the tears as several others in the group build a makeshift shelter.

Not everyone is faring so well. Maurice, one of the older members of the group, begins to scream and shout. His eyes are wide and bloodshot, and his gaze seems … distant. He starts to run down the mountain slope, cursing and wailing. Hassan tries to take him by the arm, but Maurice—bigger and stronger—easily breaks free, shouting something about, "They are coming!"

You don't know Maurice well, but he's the strongest person in the group, and you need him. You stand up and start to follow, but Hassan grabs you by the arm. "I think he's having some sort of breakdown," he explains. "I don't think you can help him. It's not safe."

To follow Hassan's advice, go to page 33.
To go after Maurice, turn to page 97.

Hassan is right. Maurice is not in his right mind. You can only watch as he disappears over the horizon. You hold out hope that he'll return, but he never does.

The days and weeks that follow are a blur. The skies fill with a dense blanket of dust and clouds. Temperatures plummet. Violent earthquakes shake the land. Through it all, you stick with the group. Hassan leads you south along the western side of the mountains. To the east, the devastation is staggering. The wave has scoured the earth, stripping down buildings, trees—everything. What little survives is quickly killed off by the sulfuric acid rain that seems to fall all day, every day. It looks like something out of a science fiction movie.

Turn the page.

In time, a split in the group emerges. Hassan wants to continue south, fearing that temperatures are only going to continue to fall. Another young woman, Jennifer, wants to strike west. "To the heartland," she says, reasoning that the center of the continent will be the most stable.

To stay with Hassan and continue south, turn to page 80.
To strike west with Jennifer, turn to page 82.

More than a hundred miles in a day, when you're already feeling sick and exhausted? You don't think you can do it. You wish your new friends well and head southwest toward the Blue Ridge Mountains.

You sleep a few hours in an abandoned barn. Then you're back on the road at dawn. At one point, you hear gunfire ahead of you. Hassan was right—some would kill for your bike. You resolve to keep off road as much as possible. It slows you down, but one look at the looming mountains tells you that time is growing less critical with every passing mile.

It's late afternoon when you reach Shenandoah National Park. The main road is a parking lot. Blaring car horns and angry shouting fills the air. You stay clear, sticking to horse trails and walking paths.

Dusk approaches as you walk your bike up a steep dirt trail. Only hours until impact now. You head up one of the park's many peaks. You hear voices ahead.

To walk toward the voices, turn to page 53.
To stay away from the voices, turn to page 78.

You can't catch another glance of the figure in the floral-print dress. You sigh disappointedly and keep moving.

The White House is on lockdown. It's swarming with military personnel. You and Ed are stopped long before you arrive at the normal checkpoint. But he flashes his badge and you're behind the gates in no time.

Turn the page.

"Thanks for your help, kid," says Ed. "Look, the president was in China when the news of the asteroid broke. The vice president is staying here. As Speaker, I'm third in line. That means they want me somewhere else … somewhere safe. In a few hours, I'll be on an airplane bound for Colorado. There's a bunker there, stocked to supply more than a hundred people for years. It was built for a nuclear attack, but it should serve us well in this crisis too. I know you have your heart set on searching for your parents, but I'm sure I can get one more person on that flight. We're going to need young, strong people who are willing to lend a hand. What do you say?"

To take the offer, turn to page 61.
To decline and continue your search for your parents, turn to page 65.

"Come on, let's go," you say. "We won't get far until you get some help."

Helping Rasheed is a long, painful process. You use a T-shirt to wrap Rasheed's leg to stop the bleeding. Then you have to all but carry him up to the road. His leg is in terrible shape, and he can't put any weight on it.

It takes more than three hours, but the two of you manage to hobble back to Warrenton. You're in luck—the hospital is on the west end of town, just off the highway. But when you get there, you find out it's abandoned. A sign hangs on the main doors: "Gone west. Get to high ground. Good luck to us all."

You watch Rasheed's shoulders slump. He's running on fumes, and you're not sure how much longer you can keep him on his feet. And without a doctor, you don't have a prayer of getting the both of you to high ground.

Rasheed returns your look. He knows what you're thinking. "You tried," he says, his voice quivering.

To stay with Rasheed, turn to page 44.
To leave Rasheed and try to save yourself, turn to page 48.

"I don't really want to go east either," you say. "Let's get you to Amissville and see if there's any help there."

You use some of your drinking water to rinse Rasheed's wound. Then you tightly wrap a spare T-shirt around it to stop the bleeding. "Okay, let's move," you say, carefully helping him up.

You soon realize that it won't be that easy. Rasheed can't put any weight on his leg. Even standing upright, leaning against you, he gets lightheaded. You have to leave the bike behind, with no way to get him onto it.

The going is painfully slow. Amissville is just a few miles up the road, but it takes you many hours to cover the distance. The sun sets long before you get there. By the time you step into the little community, it's close to midnight. Even in the dark, you can see there's not much here. No hospital, no doctor's office that you can see. You knock on the doors of random houses, desperate for help. But nobody answers.

Turn the page.

"Nobody left," Rasheed says. "They've all gone for high ground, I'm sure."

Rasheed is staying brave, but you can tell he is exhausted. He can't go any farther. You find a house with the front door open and let yourselves inside. You help Rasheed down onto an old leather sofa, then flop down onto the floor next to him. You fall asleep almost immediately.

When you wake, your stomach roiling, the clock reads 9:01 a.m. You feel a chill. Exactly 12 hours until impact. "Get up, Rasheed," you call out, shaking the boy's arm. "We have to go."

But Rasheed won't wake up. His breathing is shallow and his skin is waxy. Large black circles surround his eyes. You shake him, scream at him, even slap him hard across the face, but nothing you do rouses him. He has fallen into a coma. You can't help him.

To go on alone, turn to page 43.
To stay with Rasheed until the end, turn to page 98.

Choking back tears, you cover Rasheed with a warm blanket and say your goodbyes. There's no time for sentiment—you've got 12 hours and a lot of ground to cover. You push yourself hard, heading west. But you've lost too much time, and you have to make frequent stops with an upset stomach. You watch as the sun begins to set in the west behind the Blue Ridge Mountains. They look so close, but you know they're much too far away. You're not going to make it.

Turn to page 74.

"We're not giving up that easily," you say, helping Rasheed to his feet. The two of you hobble into town. The streets are empty. It feels like a ghost town.

"Over there!" Rasheed cries, pointing to a nearby corner. Somebody's here!

"Hello!" you call, waving your arms. The figure turns, then starts heading in your direction. It's an elderly man walking with a wooden cane. His skin is wrinkled, but his eyes remain lively.

You introduce yourselves. "My friend hurt his leg. We're trying to find a doctor."

"Name's Roger," the man says. "Don't think you're likely to find a proper doctor here. Everyone left."

"Why didn't you leave?" Rasheed asks.

The man smiles. "I'm 92 years old," he says. "It's all I can do to take my morning walk anymore. If the world ends tomorrow, I'll go out with my dignity, in the comfort of my own home. Now, to your problem. Come with me."

Turn the page.

You follow Roger several blocks to a small building. "It's a veterinary clinic," Roger announces proudly. "This is my daughter's practice. It was mine before that. Now come on in and let's get you patched up."

You can't help but admire the man as he gently tends to Rasheed's broken leg. His hands tremble and his movements are slow and deliberate, but Roger manages to set the bone and craft a makeshift cast to keep the bone in place. It's dark by the time Roger is finished. You have to spend the night. At sunrise, you wake up Rasheed. "Time to go."

Roger has one more surprise for you. He hands you a key. "A mile west of town there's a horse farm," he says. "This key will get you into the barn. Now go."

With a cast and a crutch, Rasheed moves a lot better. Yet it's still slow going as the two of you hobble out of town on a dusty road. Rasheed struggles with the crutches, and he's still in a lot of pain. But you're finally moving, and it almost feels good. The birds are singing, and the notion that everything you see will be wiped away in half a day seems surreal.

You find the farm and let yourselves into the barn. Half a dozen horses graze in a fenced area attached to the barn.

"Look at that," Rasheed says, pointing to a corner in the barn. It's a four-wheeler. The paint is chipped and the seats are torn, but it might be even better than a horse—if it starts.

To use the horses to escape, turn to page 55.
To try the four-wheeler instead, turn to page 75.

"Go," says Rasheed. "I was dead the minute I fell off that bike."

With a squeeze of his arm, you're off. You waste no time—the sun has already set. Less than 24 hours until impact! In 30 minutes, you cover the distance it took the two of you hours to travel. In the dark, you search the ditch, desperately looking for the bike. Ten minutes pass. Then twenty. You begin to panic, and you're almost ready to give up the search when you see it.

You're already completely exhausted as you climb on and begin to pedal. The front rim is bent, making it wobble a bit. But the bike is otherwise in good shape. You focus all your energy on your destination—Shenandoah National Park. You stop to spend a restless night under the stars. You're back on the bike at dawn, but the going is slow. Your stomach roils, and you have to stop to throw up twice.

Shortly before noon, you find yourself back on the main road at the foot of the Blue Ridge Mountains. Traffic is at a standstill. People sit on the hoods of their cars. Others have abandoned their vehicles and continued on foot. You get more than a few jealous looks as you speed by on your bike.

"Hey kid!" a voice shouts. "Hold up a second!"

It's a young man. He's sitting on the hood of a red sports car. You almost laugh at the sight—the car is probably worth a hundred thousand dollars or more, but now it's worthless. The roads are jammed, and they're not going to open up.

"I'll give you 20,000 dollars for that bike," the man offers. He waves a wad of green in the air. It's more money than you've ever seen in your life. You smile at him, open your mouth, and shout your answer.

To say "No chance!" turn to page 51.
To say "Deal!" turn to page 52.

Twenty thousand dollars is a lot of money, but you're not sure it'll be worth the paper it's printed on after the asteroid strikes. "Sorry," you tell him, speeding away as quickly as you can. You want to put some distance between you and him, just in case he has ideas about taking the bike instead of buying it.

You veer from the main road, sticking to walking trails, bike paths, and horse paths. The grade grows steeper and steeper, and your legs ache from the effort. But one glance at the sky shows you the sun is about to set. That means time is getting very, very short.

You pick a path that is supposed to lead to one of the park's many peaks. The sky begins to dim as you walk your bike up a steep dirt trail. Just over an hour until impact now. You hear voices ahead.

To approach the voices, turn to page 53.
To avoid them, turn to page 78.

"Twenty thousand?" you repeat. You're all but sure that dollar signs are lighting up in your eyes. "Sold!"

The man smirks as he hands over the wad of cash. "Keep the car too, kid." You feel a pang of regret as you watch him disappear down a bike trail.

You stare at the bills in your hand. What are you going to do with this much money? But as cell phones and video games dance through your head, reality slaps you in the face. Civilization is about to end. Money isn't going to be anything more than paper.

"I think I just screwed up," you mutter to yourself.

You spend the next two hours slogging your way up the Blue Ridge on foot. You come across a sign reading "Elevation: 2,500 feet" as sunset approaches. That's when you take a crooked step on a rock and twist your ankle. It's not broken, but your night of climbing is over. You realize you won't be safe at 2,500 feet. You sealed your fate the minute you gave up your bike. With a sigh, you slump down onto a slick rock.

Turn to page 74.

You haven't spoken to anyone in a long time. If the end of the world is at hand, you don't want to be alone. You follow the trail to an opening, where three young women sit eating energy bars and listening to a news broadcast on a small radio.

"Hello," you call.

They appear startled at first, but when they see that you're young and alone, they warm quickly. They introduce themselves as Alisha, Tonya, and Susan. They're college roommates, all far from home.

"What are they saying?" you ask, pointing to the radio.

"They've pinned down where it's going to hit," says Alisha. "A few hundred miles south of Iceland. The scientists don't all agree on how big the wave will be. But it will be big. Close to a mile high."

Turn the page.

"We need to get to the top of this mountain then," you say.

"I don't think so," says Tonya. "My map says this mountain is 3,700 feet at its peak. We're going to try to push on down the ridge to Hawksbill. That's over 4,000 feet high. It's our best shot, but it's still another five miles, as the crow flies. This is our last rest. We're hiking nonstop until we get there. Only bad news is that we have to go down before we go up again. Want to join us?"

Five miles of mountain terrain, and you're already exhausted. That might be tough to pull off even if you were rested. You can be on top of this peak in 30 minutes. But then, another 300 feet of elevation could be the difference between life and death.

To join the young women bound for Hawksbill,
turn to page 59.
To continue up the slope on your own, turn to page 78.

"That thing's in rough shape," you say. "Let's stick with the plan."

You're lucky. The horses are very tame and gentle. You saddle up a pair of brown mares, help Rasheed up onto his, then mount your own. "Years of watching cowboy movies are finally paying off," you say with a smile.

Soon you're on the open road. The horses move along at a healthy canter. By noon, you're at the foot of the mountains. A sign reading Shenandoah National Park stands before you. A large map of the park shows your location.

"If we follow the Allegheny Path, we can get to one of these peaks," Rasheed says, pointing at the ridge.

Turn the page.

The traffic on Skyline Drive, the main road through the park, is at a standstill. But on horseback, you aren't dependent on paved roads. You follow the trail higher and higher. As evening sets in, you follow a sign to Stony Man Horse Trail. Stony Man is a peak standing more than 4,000 feet above sea level. You lead the horses all the way to the top.

It's as far as you can go. You help Rasheed off his horse, taking care not to put any weight on his leg. His face shows a lot of pain, but he hasn't complained once. Together, you sit and watch the sun set. "Premium seating for the end of the world," Rasheed says.

Turn the page.

He's right. You never see the asteroid, but the eastern sky lights up. The entire planet seems to tremble. Over the terrifying, awe-inspiring minutes that follow, you see and feel it all—the shock wave, the gusting winds, the fiery debris raining down from the sky. But the giant wave is the sight you'll never forget. It's like a living thing, swallowing everything in its path. It comes fast, pushing a blast of wind in front of it.

Rasheed screams. Your heart feels like it might beat right out of your chest as you watch. The tremendous roar of the wave surrounds you and wind whips across your face. You watch the wave slam into the ridge, erasing the lower peaks in an instant and speeding closer ... closer. The two of you huddle there, clinging to each other, waiting for the end. But the end doesn't come. The wave rips out trees and rocks below you, but you're just high enough—a few hundred feet lower and you'd be dead. A moment ago, you were sitting on a mountain peak. Now it's an island.

Turn to page 90.

You sigh and nod your head. "Let's go."

The sun sinks in the sky as you, Alisha, Tonya, and Susan navigate the narrow dirt trail. You're headed down, and that makes you panic. You can't help but look up at the sky, half expecting to see something. But it looks like any other evening. You look down on the lush Linville Gorge below. The stunning, rolling hills are blanketed with lush vegetation.

And it'll all be gone in a couple of hours. As 9 p.m. approaches, you feel a renewed sense of urgency. You follow the trail as it weaves up Hawksbill. The pace is brisk, or more accurately, frantic. Your calves and thighs ache, but you ignore them.

The ground shakes. Rocks tumble down from above. You all stop for a moment, everyone holding their breath. Tonya glances at her watch. "That was it."

"How long do we have?" you ask.

"Can't be sure. Not long. The tsunami will be moving at hundreds of miles per hour."

Turn the page.

No one says another word. You're practically sprinting up the trail for Hawksbill's rocky peak. The sun has set and it's growing darker. Tonya and Alisha are falling behind, but you can't stop to help.

The ground shakes again. Earthquakes. Winds blast over the mountains. Flaming debris screams down from the sky.

You can see the rocky peak when the wave hits. The massive wall of water engulfs everything in its path. You can feel it, hear it, and smell it. You sprint and climb with every ounce of strength you have left, finally collapsing onto a rock slab next to Susan.

The sound of the wave all around you is deafening. But you're high enough—barely. Fifty feet lower and the water would have swallowed you. Tonya and Alisha weren't so lucky.

Hawksbill is no longer a mountain, though. For now, until the water recedes, it is an island. And the two of you are stranded on it.

Turn to page 90.

How can you turn down a chance to survive? "I don't know how to thank you, Ed."

Within an hour, you're seated on an Air Force Boeing C-32. You're in the air when the asteroid hits. You watch in horror on a television screen as a satellite image shows a small, bright dot over Europe that grows larger and brighter. Then the feed flickers and goes black. Impact.

The cabin of the plane remains eerily silent until the shock wave hits. For a few minutes, the aircraft rocks and dips violently as the pilots battle the extreme turbulence. But other than that, you feel strangely removed from the terror below. Here in the sky, it almost feels more like a movie than real life.

That sense quickly disappears when the plane touches down on a remote Colorado airstrip. The sky is streaked with tiny falling stars—debris from the impact re-entering Earth's atmosphere. As you stare up at the sky, a hand firmly grasps your shoulder. It's Ed. "Come on kid, let's go."

Turn the page.

The bunker itself is a marvel. Buried hundreds of feet below Earth's surface, it was designed for a nuclear attack. Television feeds show some of the devastation. A remote camera at the White House broadcasts the enormous wave that is swallowing the entire East Coast. The wall of water comes shockingly fast, and in a moment, the camera blinks out. Gone. You shiver and drop your head into your hands. You tell yourself that it's possible your parents made it out. But you don't really believe it.

For the next five years, you and the others remained safely locked underground. Through feeds to surviving cameras on the surface and satellites in space, you're able to watch the amazing and terrible transformation of the planet. Enormous clouds of dust shroud the world, casting it into a dull darkness. Little can grow with the lack of direct sunlight. Plants and animals die off from the cold and lack of food. Yet below ground, in the bunker, you are safe.

Turn the page.

Five years after impact, Ed gathers the survivors, who are like family to you now. "As you know, we had five years worth of food and water in the bunker," Ed says. "Those stores are beginning to run out. We knew the day would come, and it's here. It's time to return to the surface, to try to reclaim the planet. The nuclear winter is finally starting to lift. Sunshine is once again finding its way to the planet's surface. It will be hard, but we have to try."

Ed's plan is to return to Washington, D.C. Most of the survivors plan to join him. A second, smaller group is heading to Kansas, with the hopes to start a new farming community.

**To go with Ed back to Washington, D.C.,
turn to page 93.
To join the group bound for Kansas, turn to page 96.**

"I'm sorry, I have to find my parents."

Ed gazes at you sadly but doesn't try to change your mind. "Come to the White House gate if you find them or change your mind." He tears a badge off his jacket. "Give them this. We'll be leaving in about an hour."

You shake his hand and watch as he disappears behind a tall gate. You rush back toward the Washington Monument, scanning the crowd. At first it seems hopeless. But then you see it—the dress. You call out "Mom!" and rush after the woman.

Turn to page 91.

The barn is abandoned and unlocked. You flop down on some old hay, and you're snoring within minutes. It's rest you badly needed.

You're back on the road by dawn. You push yourself hard throughout the day, but as you gaze ahead, everything starts to feel helpless. You're almost there, but there's just no way you'll get high enough in time.

Around 6 p.m., a distant sound catches your attention. Thump, thump, thump. You scan the sky, searching. Then you see it. A helicopter! Frantically, you leap, wave, and shout. And to your shock, it works! The helicopter veers toward you, then slowly settles down onto a flat area. It's motor whines to a stop.

The words NEWS 5 are painted onto the side of the chopper. The lone pilot waves you in. You don't waste a second.

Turn the page.

"Jim," says the pilot, extending a hand. "I'm the traffic reporter for News 5." You introduce yourself, unable to believe your luck. Your eyes well with tears.

You strap in as the chopper rises up above the ground and banks west. Jim smiles. "I should warn you though, I'm not really a pilot. I've spent enough time in one of these watching, though. I know enough to handle the basics. And, well … this chopper is technically stolen. When I realized that there was no other way out, I just sort of took it. I wasn't planning to stop to pick anyone up, but … I guess guilt got the best of me."

You wave your hand. "Fine by me, Jim. I figured I was a goner until I saw you. Now … well at least we've got a fighting chance."

Jim guides the helicopter over the Blue Ridge. Below, you see pockets of people. They wave and shout, pleading for Jim to stop. But even if there was room for all of them in the helicopter, there's nowhere to put the chopper down.

"We'll go west until she's out of fuel," Jim says. "No idea where we go after that. But it's a better plan than sitting around waiting for the wave."

You clear the Blue Ridge and soar over the Allegheny Mountains. You're in the air somewhere over Ohio when the asteroid hits. The eastern sky lights up. Soon after, the shock wave hits. The blast of wind slams into the chopper with frightening power. Jim isn't buckled in, and the jolt slams his head into the cockpit window. The sick thud leaves little doubt—he's almost certainly dead. You'll worry about Jim later, though. The chopper, tossed and turned by the violent shock wave, is falling fast.

To brace for impact, turn to page 70.
To unbuckle and try to take over the aircraft's controls, turn to page 101.

You realize the terrifying truth. The helicopter is going down, and there's nothing you can do about it. Your entire world is spinning, faster, faster. You brace your arms, hold your breath, and close your eyes as the ground below grows closer ... closer ... closer ....

You black out. When you come to, the helicopter is on the ground. Jim's limp body lies against the shattered door. The angle of his neck confirms he's dead. You unhook your harness and crawl from the wreckage.

The earth shakes beneath your feet. The night sky is streaked with flaming debris, coming back down to Earth. You walk until you see a sign: Columbus: 32 miles.

You're alone, bleeding, and miles from the nearest city. All around you, the world is falling apart. To the east, a giant wave is swallowing the entire east coast at this very moment. Yet here you are, alive.

You start walking. Maybe things will be better in Columbus.

THE END

To follow another path, turn to page 10.
To learn more about asteroids, turn to page 103.

With a sigh, you lay the bike down on the road. It carried you a lot of the miles you needed to make. But now it's back to your own two feet, and that means there's no time for sleep.

You walk through the night. There's no moon in the sky, making for a very dark, eerie march. By 3 a.m., you feel like a zombie. You're almost sleepwalking, only dimly aware of your own left-right-left-right rhythm.

When one of your steps goes wrong, you're suddenly alert again. Your ankle turns and makes a sickening snap. You collapse onto the dirt road in a heap, shouting out in pain.

The ankle is broken. You drag yourself off of the road, to the trunk of a tree that sits along a fence line.

Turn the page.

You're helpless. The sun rises in the sky, but you're stuck. Mid-morning, a family with two young kids passes you on foot. The mother starts to offer you their help, but the father quickly cuts her off. "Best of luck," he says before the family disappears down the road. You can't blame them. They may not have time to reach safety as it is. Stopping to help you would probably doom them.

You sleep on and off much of the day, already resigned to your fate. As evening approaches, you're almost eager to get the show started.

Turn to page 74.

You sit alone, gazing at the sky. Right on the edge of the horizon, one bright star grows brighter and larger by the second. Of course, it's no star at all. It dips below the horizon, hidden from view. All you can do is wait.

You glance at your watch. 9:01. The sky lights up bright orange, and the earth shakes. The shock wave hits you a few minutes later. The wind howls. The earth continues to quiver. And that is just the beginning.

You hear the wave long before you see it. The noise, like a neverending roar of thunder, fills the air. In the eastern sky, a massive wall of darkness wipes out the orange glow, the stars, everything.

The mile-high tsunami swallows the land whole. It's like the sea itself is rising up. You only have a few seconds to marvel at it and wonder how anyone could survive it. The speed and power of the wave crushes and drowns everything in its path. Your story has ended, but for the people left, the nightmare is only beginning.

THE END

To follow another path, turn to page 10.
To learn more about asteroids, turn to page 103.

Horses would be good, but nothing can beat a four-wheeler. After a few minutes of fiddling, you get the vehicle started. The engine sputters, chugs, and smokes. "Probably just some old fuel in the line," Rasheed says.

You find a spare can of gasoline and climb on. Rasheed sits behind you. "Let's go!"

You take it slow at first, fearing that a rough ride will hurt Rasheed's leg. But after several miles, he taps you on the shoulder. "Stop driving like my grandma," he says. "We're kind of on a deadline here!"

With a grin, you gun it. The engine races ... then sputters ... then dies with a pop and a puff of smoke. No matter what you do, you can't get it to start again.

You're stuck in the middle of nowhere, still dozens of miles from the mountains. You don't have the heart to turn around and head east again, back to the horse farm. So you press on. Rasheed pushes himself to his limits, but he's still slowing you down.

Turn the page.

The sun dips below the mountains in the west. They look so close, but they might as well be a world away. The last glow of daylight is fading from the sky when the two of you finally stop.

You never see the asteroid, but you feel it hit. The ground quivers. The eastern sky glows orange. For a moment, everything is eerily quiet. Then the shock wave hits. Debris streams through the sky—rocks and dust thrown up into the atmosphere during impact. It's a fireworks show unlike anything you'd ever imagined.

The tsunami hardly seems like a wave at all. Somehow you expected a towering crest, like a giant version of what you see in surfing videos. What you can see in the fading light looks more like a black wall of water, swallowing up everything in its path.

You give Rasheed's hand a squeeze. "Thanks," he says a moment before the wave strikes. "I'm glad I wasn't alone." You agree.

THE END

To follow another path, turn to page 10.
To learn more about asteroids, turn to page 103.

You're on your own, and you don't want anyone else slowing you down. You hope for the best for everyone, but you can only look out for yourself right now. Your goal remains the top of this mountain.

It's a tough trek up, and by the time you reach the peak, the sun is beginning to set. When you finally reach the peak, you see a middle-aged couple on a rock outcropping, staring to the east. They turn as you approach. The woman gestures to the rock next to her.

"Where is everyone?" you ask, plopping down on the rock. The man points west. "Most headed farther inland," he says. "We would have too, but this is as far as we could make it."

A small FM radio sits between the couple. The news is grim. The wave will be close to a mile high. It will wash hundreds of miles inland. Suddenly, a pop of static hisses through the small speakers. The broadcast goes dead. Moments later, the eastern sky glows orange, and the earth trembles. Your watch reads 9:01.

"How high are we?" you ask.

"My map says 3,700 feet," says the woman. "We're just hoping that's high enough."

You do your best to hold on when the earthquakes and rockslides start. Flaming debris falls from the sky, and lightning strikes from every direction. It's terrifying, but it doesn't come close to the horror that follows. Even as you cling to the ground with everything around you falling apart, your breath catches in your throat as the giant wall of water rises above you. The wave rolls over the land at hundreds of miles per hour, engulfing everything in its path—including you.

THE END

To follow another path, turn to page 10.
To learn more about asteroids, turn to page 103.

The air grows colder every day. Hassan has gotten the group this far—you're not going to give up on him now. After a tearful farewell, Jennifer and several others strike west.

As your group moves into lower elevations, the devastation grows worse and worse. Your stomach growls as your food stores dwindle. You trudge through the layer of sodden mud that coats the entire landscape.

The land is barren. Nothing of civilization survived the wave. Your group turns west, searching for land untouched by the tsunami. Early one morning, a familiar whoosh-whoosh-whoosh sound approaches over the horizon.

"Helicopter!" shouts Hassan.

The aircraft passes almost directly overhead. You wave and shout and jump, desperate for rescue. But the chopper never even slows down. Dejected, you watch it disappear over the western horizon.

Hassan collapses later that morning and passes out. Without leadership, the group fractures. You're the only one to stay with Hassan. That evening, he takes his final breath. You sit alone, over his body, numb to everything that has happened.

You gaze over the landscape, like some alien world. No help is coming. You defied all odds by surviving the asteroid impact. Little did you know, surviving the broken world it left behind would be much, much harder.

THE END

To follow another path, turn to page 10.
To learn more about asteroids, turn to page 103.

The land to the south is barren. You beg Hassan to come west, but he refuses to change his mind. With a tearful goodbye, you, Jennifer, and two others strike west.

The world you find is changed forever. Fires have gutted entire towns. Acid rain has killed most of the plants. Mudslides have washed away roads and bridges. Enormous storms of and ash sweep over the land. Jennifer, who studied geology, explains that the impact likely set off huge volcanic eruptions worldwide.

By the time you reach eastern Ohio, you begin to find communities, alive and intact. South of Dayton, you pass a tiny farming town. Only about a dozen residents remain. They eagerly welcome you into their community.

"They say the sun won't shine here again for another decade," says Sandra, the little town's mayor. "But we've got a grain elevator brimming with corn and soybeans. With hard work, we can make it."

You've come this far. Maybe you *can* make it.

THE END
To follow another path, turn to page 10.
To learn more about asteroids, turn to page 103.

A glance at the crowded streets in front of you makes you realize you were foolish to believe you could find your parents. There are just too many people here, and you can't even be sure your parents are among them. Given the choice between dying alone on the streets or taking a long shot with two strangers, you decide to make a distraction.

You watch as Hank and Sean move toward the Jeep. Hank looks your way and gives a nod. That's your cue.

You rush out into the street. "Help!" you shout, frantically pointing behind you. "That man is chasing me! Help me!"

Everything happens in a blur. The soldiers step toward you as Hank vaults into the Jeep. The roar of the engine and the squealing of tires are followed by the pop-pop-pop of gunfire. You leap as the Jeep streaks by. A strong hand—Sean's—grabs you. You cling to the side of the Jeep, Sean holding you firm, as Hank weaves onto the sidewalk and street. You almost fall off as he screams around a corner, but Sean doesn't let go.

Finally, the Jeep slows enough for you to climb inside. Hank steers it down a series of alleys and side streets. "I think we did it!" he shouts, joy on his face.

You round a corner, only to come face-to-face with a tank. A voice through a megaphone warns, "Stop. This is your only warning."

Hank steps down on the gas. The Jeep's engine roars. The noise almost blocks out the chatter of machine gun fire.

The Jeep is instantly ripped to shreds, offering no protection from the hail of bullets. Your last thought is: Maybe stealing an Army Jeep wasn't such a great idea after all.

THE END

To follow another path, turn to page 10.
To learn more about asteroids, turn to page 103.

You glance at the soldiers ahead, assault rifles in their hands. "Ahh … think I'll pass on that one, Hank. Best of luck to you."

You continue toward the National Mall. The Washington Monument looms ahead. You know that's where your parents were headed. But as you look at the crowd before you—probably hundreds of thousands of people—you realize that your quest is all but hopeless.

Behind you, you hear the squealing of tires, followed immediately by gunshots and shouting. You don't turn around. *Hope you made it, Hank.*

You search for your parents for the next three hours. Fighting your way through an increasingly restless crowd is exhausting. As sunset approaches and the time of impact grows near, panic really sets in. A mob rushes the White House gates. Fights break out in the streets. You watch people looting nearby stores and can't help but wonder what they plan to do with the TVs and jewelry they're stealing.

Before you know it, it's 9:01. For a moment, the entire crowd of people seems to hold their collective breath. You can't see the asteroid, but you feel the impact. The entire Earth shudders.

Then come the earthquakes. You reach out your arms to steady yourself as the ground heaves beneath your feet. A voice shouts out. The Washington Monument is collapsing! You watch in horror as the massive structure crumbles and falls, crushing countless people below. Somewhere behind you, you hear a scream. The scream is somehow familiar.

Turn the page.

You turn. Your knees go weak as you see your parents standing there, not 25 feet from you. "Mom! Dad!" you yell as you charge through the crowd.

They're even more shocked than you are. The three of you fall to your knees on the lawn of the National Mall.

The wave will be along in minutes to wipe it all away. But for this moment, you are with the ones you love. You are happy.

THE END

To follow another path, turn to page 10.
To learn more about asteroids, turn to page 103.

It's a seemingly endless night, filled with terror. The earthquakes shake the land mercilessly. Flaming debris rains down from the sky, igniting the forest. Blazes smolder in every direction. A haze of smoke hangs in the air.

In time, the water recedes. The land below is stripped, scarred, and scattered with wreckage. Nothing survived the water—plant, animal, or human.

Yet you are alive, and you are not alone. Can you survive in this new world, far from any surviving civilization, with the sun blocked out by dust and debris?

Maybe, maybe not. But you've already beaten the odds, just by being here. You're not about to give up now.

THE END

To follow another path, turn to page 10.
To learn more about asteroids, turn to page 103.

You rush through the crowded mall, weaving through the masses. "Mom! Mom!"

No luck. The woman is gone. Was it your mother? You spend the next few hours combing through the crowd. It feels hopeless. Even if your parents are here, finding them would be like finding a needle in a haystack.

You slump down onto a bench, your head in your hands. The sun is setting behind you. That's when you hear it. It's faint at first, then louder. Someone is calling your name. You stand and turn. Two figures are rushing through the crowd.

"Dad! Mom!" Your heart leaps in your chest as your parents wrap you up in a giant hug.

After the thrill of finding each other passes, a darkness comes over your dad's face. He's furious that you came east. "We wanted to come to you, but the roads ... the crowd. Why would you come this way? The city is doomed."

Turn the page.

"I had to … I couldn't go by myself." The look in your parents' eyes is heartbreaking. You can see that they held out hope that you'd make it, and now they know differently.

"Maybe we can find an airplane … someone to fly us out of here." Your voice is growing desperate. Your dad, crying, only nods his head. He doesn't believe it any more than you do.

"Let's just keep moving. Keep trying. I don't want to just sit and wait for it," you say.

You start the journey, hand in hand with your parents. Barring some miracle, you have no chance to reach safety. But at least you'll be with the two people you love most in the world. If you've got only hours to live, you'd rather spend that time with them.

THE END

To follow another path, turn to page 10.
To learn more about asteroids, turn to page 103.

Three dozen survivors board the same C-32 that carried you from D.C. five years ago. The cross-country trip is harrowing. Everything has changed. Cities and towns lie in ruin. In places, the landscape is bare and lifeless. It looks like Earth is in the middle of an ice age.

The Washington, D.C., area is unrecognizable. The city has been wiped away by the wave. The Potomac no longer exists. Ed stands on bare rock, staring at the land. He instantly looks 10 years older. You know that his dream of restarting the government here has just died.

After a few minutes, he turns. "Okay, let's go. There's nothing left here."

But there's one big problem: The C-32 is almost out of fuel. "We won't get more than 100 miles," says Sharon, the Air Force pilot.

Turn the page.

Ed's face goes pale. You look at the people around you. Everyone was counting on finding something here … someone. Ed had been certain others would have returned. What supplies you were able to load onto the plane will last only a few weeks.

Everyone seems to be waiting for Ed to make a decision, but you can see that at this moment, he's not able. Someone else needs to step up.

"Come on, then," you say. "Let's carry what we can. It's time for a hike."

You'll go west, toward the mountains. Maybe there you can find a pocket of civilization that survived the impact and the years of horror that followed. But looking at the wasteland all around you, it's hard to get your hopes up.

THE END

To follow another path, turn to page 10.
To learn more about asteroids, turn to page 103.

With a tearful farewell, you say goodbye to Ed and his group—all of whom have become like family since the disaster. You wave as the C-32 rises into the sky once again, then disappears over the eastern horizon. You and the remaining survivors pack what supplies you can and load it onto military jeeps.

The overland trip is both fascinating and horrifying. Fires have wiped out large tracts of forested land. Acid rain has left behind patchy wastelands. Yet you also see signs of hope. Planted fields. Communities. People have survived the nightmare. Not many, but some.

When you arrive in Kansas, the real work begins. Working as a group, you till and plant, irrigate and fertilize. You've got the best genetically modified plants to work with. They are designed to thrive in low sunlight and acidic soil. As you gaze at the young seedlings pushing their way through the cracked ground, you're filled with hope.

THE END

To follow another path, turn to page 10.
To learn more about asteroids, turn to page 103.

"I have to try," you explain. Hassan lets go of your arm reluctantly. You rush down the slope after Maurice. The sky above you lights up with falling debris. Something slams into the ground only a few hundred feet from you, instantly igniting a stand of trees.

By the time you reach Maurice, he has collapsed onto the ground. He lies there, sobbing uncontrollably. Carefully, you reach out to touch his shoulder. The big man twists and grabs your arm with alarming speed. His grip is painfully tight, and his eyes are full of fire.

"Whoa, there," you say. Keeping your voice low and calm. But you realize there's nothing you can do. All you want is to be back with your group.

The sky is filled with chunks of rock, thrown up into space by the impact, then crashing back down to Earth. The one that hits you is no bigger than a softball, but at such incredible speed, you never stand a chance. You fall to the ground instantly, your journey at an end.

THE END

To follow another path, turn to page 10.
To learn more about asteroids, turn to page 103.

You can't bring yourself to leave. You've known Rasheed less than a day, but he feels like the only person in the world you have left. You spend the day by his side, desperately hoping for a miracle. Maybe … just maybe … he'll wake up, you tell yourself.

But by sunset, Rasheed's breathing is very shallow. You refuse to let him be alone in his final moments … your final moments. A glance at a clock tells you that it's time … 9:01. You hold your breath, waiting, watching out the window.

It starts with a bright orange glow over the eastern horizon, followed by an incredible trembling. For a few short moments, it's almost beautiful. You find yourself staring at what appears something like a brilliant sunrise. But the moment passes when the shock wave—a wall of air pushed out by the immense impact—strikes. The house rattles. Pictures fall off the walls. You hear the sound of glass breaking from the kitchen. A tree limb smashes through the roof in one of the bedrooms.

Turn the page.

The sky lights up with shooting stars—bits of rock thrown up into space that are falling back down to Earth. Again, if you ignore everything else, it's beautiful.

Then, the orange glow in the east slowly disappears as a wall of water a mile high towers like a great rushing mountain, bearing down on the entire East Coast. This is anything but beautiful. You don't want to see it. Instead, you take Rasheed's hand and close your eyes, glad that you're not alone here at the end.

THE END

To follow another path, turn to page 10.
To learn more about asteroids, turn to page 103.

The helicopter is going down fast. You reach down, fumbling with your straps. After several terrifying moments, you free yourself from your harness and slide over to the controls, jamming yourself up against Jim's limp body.

You grab the stick to try to steer the chopper. Frantically, you pull back, hoping that will bring the aircraft up. But the helicopter is spinning out of control. Out the cockpit window, you see the ground growing closer ... closer.

You flick switches. You jam the stick left and right. But it's hopeless. You scream in the last moment, realizing that without your harness, your story ends here.

THE END

To follow another path, turn to page 10.
To learn more about asteroids, turn to page 103.

LOOKING UP

It's extremely unlikely that you'd hear about a massive asteroid or comet that is going to hit Earth tomorrow. Our modern warning systems should spot a large asteroid with advance warning. But scientists think that a major impact is a virtual certainty to happen again—even if it could be millions of years in the future. With all the rocks flying around our solar system, it's only a matter of time until one is on a collision course with Earth.

Just what are asteroids and comets? They're some of the material left over after the formation of the solar system. Asteroids are found throughout the solar system, but they are most common in the Asteroid Belt between the orbits of Mars and Jupiter. Asteroids are big, heavy, metal-rich chunks of rock. The biggest asteroid is Ceres at 590 miles (950 kilometers) across! Ceres is so big that some consider it a minor planet.

Comets start out in a place called the Oort cloud, far beyond the orbits of any of the planets. A little nudge from the gravity of a passing star or other astronomical body can send comets hurtling into the inner solar system. These balls of rock and ice turn into giant bullets headed toward the sun.

Earth is pelted by little asteroids every day. Most burn up in the atmosphere before reaching Earth's surface. Every hundred years or so, a bigger one plows into the planet, causing local damage. And perhaps once every 100 million years, a giant asteroid or comet causes a global catastrophe. The last one hit about 66 million years ago. Many scientists think it's what wiped out the dinosaurs.

The asteroid described in this story slammed into the ocean. What happens next? The impact vaporizes the seawater underneath it. It slams down onto the ocean floor, with the force of the blast hurling tons of rock back up into the sky. Anything within hundreds of miles of the blast will be dead instantly.

Then a shock wave travels through the air. Meanwhile, the water that has been pushed away from the impact site rushes back in to fill the hole. This forms an enormous tsunami—actually, a whole series of them! Scientists disagree on how big an impact tsunami could get. Some think that it could be a mile high or more. Others think that the wave would collapse on itself before reaching such heights. In any case, a series of these waves would rush out from the impact zone. Coastal areas worldwide would be swallowed.

Earth itself would be left reeling. The tectonic plates would be thrown out of balance. Terrible earthquakes and volcanic eruptions would follow. Debris launched into the sky would begin to rain down, setting fires worldwide. Ash and dust would fill the sky, blocking out sunlight and causing a nuclear winter that would kill off plants and animals. With food sources gone, few large land animals would have much chance of survival—humans included.

It's a grim forecast. Yet there's hope. Astronomers have tracked and catalogued many of the solar system's largest asteroids and comets. They can calculate exactly where they'll be and when. Good news: They haven't found anything that's likely to hit Earth for a very long time.

So what if astronomers do discover a space rock on a crash course with Earth? With enough warning, we may have a chance to divert it. Scientists have come up with all kinds of ideas. One is to focus the sun's rays to superheat parts of the asteroid. This would cause some of the rock to vaporize and vent, which could change the rock's course just enough to miss Earth. Others have suggested attaching huge solar sails to an asteroid, or even blowing it up or deflecting it with nuclear blasts!

It all sounds incredible, yet the science is real. The consequences, if such an impact did happen, would be catastrophic. It's a good reason to continue looking to the skies—just in case.

SURVIVAL REFERENCE GUIDE

In this story, humanity had little warning that a massive asteroid was about to strike. In real life, we could have months or even years of advanced warning before such a massive strike. That's plenty of time for you to gather your own personal survival kit. Here's a few items that can give you a better chance of surviving the doomsday event:

SURVIVAL KIT

*A weather-proof, radiation-proof, earthquake-proof, high-elevation bunker

*Canned food or dehydrated food (high-protein options like beans and tuna)

*Lots of bottled water

*A first-aid kit

*A battery-operated short-wave radio

*A wind turbine; solar panels will be worthless in a nuclear winter

*Breathing masks—it's going to be dusty for a while!

*A good telescope—you might as well get a good look at the end of the world!

TEN THINGS TO REMEMBER DURING AN ASTEROID STRIKE

- **Know where the asteroid is going to hit.** Stay clear of the impact area.

- **Get away from the coasts.** Oceans cover two-thirds of the Earth's surface. That makes an ocean strike likely. A large strike will create a series of tsunamis that will strike every coast on Earth. Move inland and get to high ground.

- **Bring warm clothing.** A massive asteroid strike will blanket Earth in ash and dust. The sun may not shine for years or decades. That's a lot of winter. Dress accordingly.

- **Desperate times call for desperate measures.** You won't be the only one trying to stock up and survive. Beware of strangers. Hide your supplies and don't tell anyone where they are.

- **Learn a trade.** To survive a world after impact, find a useful trade. Train to be a doctor, carpenter, mason, or mechanic. The new world won't need stockbrokers or advertising reps for awhile.

- **Save pennies, not paper.** Paper money is likely to be worthless in the post-impact world. Metals such as gold, silver, and copper will be king again. Pennies and nickels might even be worth more than $100 bills.

- **Don't be a lone ranger.** If you're going to survive the aftermath of a massive impact, you're not going to do it alone. Seek out others. Communities have a much better chance of making it than individuals.

- **Earth will move.** You can't smash one giant rock into another without some consequences. A large asteroid strike is going to rattle Earth's tectonic plates. That means earthquakes, volcano eruptions, and tsunamis.

- **Bring an umbrella.** Everything that gets tossed up into the atmosphere and space comes back down eventually. The big stuff smashes back down to Earth. A lot of the dust will, in time, come down with the rain. That will be acid rain, so don't try to catch a drop on your tongue.

- **Don't give up.** As long as you're drawing breath, you've got a chance. Keep doing all you can to survive.

GLOSSARY

ACID RAIN (A-suhd RAYNE)—rain that is acidic from pollutants in the air

ASTEROID (AS-tuh-royd)—a small, rocky body orbiting the sun

ATMOSPHERE (AT-muhss-feehr)—the layer of air that surrounds a planet or moon

BUNKER (BUHNG-kuhr)—a reinforced underground shelter, often used for surviving disasters

COMA (KOH-muh)—a prolonged state of deep unconsciousness

COMET (KOM-uht)—a celestial object consisting of a nucleus of ice and dust

FERTILIZE (FUHR-tuh-lyz)—to provide plants with nutrients that promote growth

GENETICALLY MODIFIED (juh-NET-uh-kuh-lee MAH-duh-fyed)—having DNA altered by humans to produce a desired trait, such as drought resistance in crops

IRRIGATE (IHR-uh-gate)—to water

NUCLEAR WINTER (NOO-klee-ur WIN-tuhr)—a period of abnormal cold and darkness caused by a layer of smoke and dust in the atmosphere that blocks the sun's rays

OORT CLOUD (ORT KLOWD)—a spherical cloud that surrounds the sun, and from which comets originate

TSUNAMI (soo-NAH-mee)—a long, high sea wave caused by a disturbance such as an earthquake

ORBIT (OR-bit)—the path one astronomical body takes around a larger body

SOLAR SYSTEM (SOH-lur SISS-tuhm)—the Sun and all of the bodies that orbit it, including planets, moons, asteroids, and comets

TECTONIC PLATES (tek-TON-ik PLAYTES)—gigantic slabs of Earth's crust that move around on magma

READ MORE

Kortenkamp, Steve. *Asteroids, Comets, and Meteoroids.* North Mankato, Minn.: Capstone Press, 2012.

Miller, Ron. *Seven Wonders of Asteroids, Comets, and Meteors.* Minneapolis: Twenty-First Century Books, 2011.

Woolf, Alex. *An Asteroid Strike.* Chicago: Heinemann Library, 2013.

INTERNET SITES

Use FactHound to find Internet sites related to this book. All of the sites on FactHound have been researched by our staff.

Here's all you do:
Visit *www.facthound.com*
Type in this code: 9781491481097

AUTHOR

Matt Doeden is the author of more than 200 children's fiction and non-fiction books. A lifelong fan of science fiction and "what if" stories, he lives in Minnesota with his wife and two children.

ILLUSTRATOR

Paul Davidson is an illustrator and comic book artist from the north of England. He has been a professional artist for more than 25 years, working with publishers from around the world. He has illustrated comics for various publishers and even tried his skills in the video games industry. He spent 9 years as a storyboard/concept artist, where he also acted as art director for several titles. In 2008, Marvel Entertainment lured him back into sequential art to draw for various X-Men related titles. Following the success of the motion picture *Dredd* in 2012, Paul was asked to draw the sequel in comic book form for *2000AD*, which has been published worldwide to critical acclaim. Paul lives by the sea and enjoys long walks on the beach with his beautiful wife and beloved dog.